Table of Contents

Parenting an Overweight Teen Isn't Easy

There are no two ways about it, being the parent of a teen can be taxing. This young person whom you've loved so much for his entire life may have suddenly changed. He may have become sullen and withdrawn, or moody and volatile. Even more difficult, he now wants to make his own decisions about where he goes and when. His life may seem like a path between school, the kitchen, and his computer, or it may seem like he doesn't go out of the house except when he absolutely has to.

If your teen is overweight, it can make this time even more difficult. The media love to tell us that parents are the reason kids get fat. This usually comes right after telling us the vast number of diseases these young people are at risk for because they're heavy. These are not just typical teen challenges. These are real problems which will haunt the kids for the rest of their lives--and parents are being told that it's our fault! So now we've got guilt for being a bad parent, guilt for "making" our kids ill, and we've got teenagers in our lives. No wonder we want to throw our hands up in defeat!

I invite you to take a couple of deep breaths and get some perspective. Remember that everything you read should be interpreted with caution. Journalists often don't get their information from the original source, and their job is to tell a story. In the process of this, they tend to make research sound like it's black and white, when it's really describing many shades of gray. Being heavy may convey health risks for some individuals, but there are also plenty of examples of very healthy people outside of the average weight range. Parents' behaviors may contribute somewhat to teen weight, but so do genes, peers, school, and so many other factors outside of your control. So remember that everyone is different, and as parents your job is to do your best to love your child and teach them that loving themselves, not perfection, is the goal.

Who's to Blame? And More Importantly, Does it Matter?

In the day to day craziness of parenting and life, it is so easy to unintentionally slip into behaviors that can contribute to our children's weight gain. In the rush of getting through the week parents sometimes fall short. A busy day at work and after school activities may mean that there's just not time to make a nutritionally balanced dinner and you just go for a quick and easy run to McDonalds. Or maybe you have your own issues with food that you may have unintentionally conveyed to your teen. Or you hate to exercise and avoid it like the plague.

Even if you have been guilty of all of these things, and therefore unintentionally may have helped create an environment for easy weight gain, I hope that I can help you relax about this. Because here's the thing--you're human. Being human means that you'll make mistakes. It also means that you have the gift of language. So if you review your parenting and see some weaknesses, you can talk to your child, and apologize for creating an environment where she turned to food for reasons other than sustenance.

Apologize to yourself, too. Raising a child is extremely hard work. To make matters worse, we live in a society that's all about food -- we're bombarded with it in advertising, at restaurants, in stores. Food is portrayed as something to be used as comfort, a special treat, or a reward. At the same time, our culture is also sending us messages about how important it is to be thin. No wonder we have a complicated relationship with food!

So if you weren't -- and still aren't -- a perfect parent, that's okay. You don't have to be. You don't expect your child to be perfect, and she doesn't expect you to be. Giving up the guilt and accepting yourself, mistakes and all, is the first step towards helping your teen love herself.

How Does Your Teen Feel her Body?

Once you've forgiven yourself for being human, your next step is to find out where your teen stands on the issue of her size. We live in a society where thin is in, and where we are exposed to mixed messages about food and body image on a daily basis. It's no wonder so many teens (and adults) feel negatively about their weight if they're not thin (and sometimes even when they are thin).

Starting this conversation with your teen may not be easy because weight is often a sensitive topic. One way to initiate this conversation is to discuss these stereotypes with your child and see what she thinks. Ask about how she feels stereotypes or weight bias have influenced her own body image. Or, if you feel comfortable, you might start out by talking about lessons you learned from your own struggles with weight and health. However you decide to approach the topic, the most important issue is to make it clear to your teen that you are providing a safe and non-judgmental space for her to talk about her feelings about weight.

It is very possible that your child is concerned about his weight. Here's where you have the chance to shine as a parent! Your child has a concern that this book will help you solve. Enjoy it – often as parents of teens the problems they have are so out of our hands that all we can do is watch and hope they will be over soon.

If your child doesn't seem to be concerned with his weight, your job gets a little more tricky. If he's just mildly overweight, then that may be fine with you. If he's not suffering, why should you be concerned? However, if your teen is severely obese, you've got a bigger battle. Life will likely be harder for him because he's heavy. If he doesn't see it and feels content with his life the way it is, it's going to be much more difficult to help him. While you may be concerned about his weight and the health or social implications that go along with it, you also don't want to betray his trust by pointing out the problem. It may help to search out a therapist who uses Motivational Interviewing[3], a non-confrontational, empathetic process that can help your teen identify his behavior and create changes for himself that can resolve destructive patterns. Sometimes having a non-parental adult to share his concerns with is the first step to helping your teen identify his problems and make a plan for change.

Supporting Change

Once you've addressed your own vulnerability and created a space for your teen to share hers, this is the moment to ask her to let you in. How can you help? Is there anything that she needs or wants from you that could help make a difference for her?

Some of the things that you might offer to do to help your child may include the following:

Buy more fresh fruit

Don't buy any sweets

Make dinner early, so late-afternoon snacking is avoided

Keep healthy snacks in the house

Make lunch so it is not necessary to eat cafeteria food

Keep water bottles handy

Help find an exercise routine

Support efforts to join a sport (transportation, equipment, etc.)

Go for a walk every night after supper

Buy a bicycle (more on that later!)

These types of supports can be huge in helping your teen's weight challenges, but be sure you don't commit to things you won't be able to do. Maybe you can't make dinner early, because you work until 6:00 every night. Your son could take over the job of cooking dinner for all of you. Whatever you decide, be sure to negotiate with your teen so that everyone is happy.

What if Your Teen Doesn't Want to Change?

If your teen denies that there is a problem and is not ready to make a change, your opportunities for helping her shed some weight are limited. Nonetheless, there are some small things that you can do to provide a healthier environment and model healthful behaviors.

Change the food you buy. Avoid purchasing sodas, sugary snacks, and high carb foods. Focus on healthy choices -- lots of fresh fruits and veggies, an assortment of cheeses and nitrate-free cold cuts, water bottles that are frosty and beckoning in the fridge. Also avoid serving (or buying) sugary desserts. A family raised on cookies may balk, but they'll get used to it. Plus, if your teen complains, you can suggest that she walk or bike to the store and purchase what she wants.

Start exercising. If your teen sees you exercising, he might decide to try it himself. It doesn't have to be a marathon, but just start getting out there. Get on a bike, and go for a ride. Take a stroll around the neighborhood. Put on a dance video and join in. Your modeling influences your teen's behavior, whether he wants to admit it or not. Invite him along - he may just surprise you and get hooked!

What About Their Health?

What Exactly is Obesity?

Children are considered obese if they are 10% above their ideal weight[4], or in the 95th percentile or above in weight[5]. Adults are considered obese if they have a BMI (Body Mass Index) of 30 or higher. The chart below gives you an approximate guide for identifying if you or your child may be overweight or obese[6].

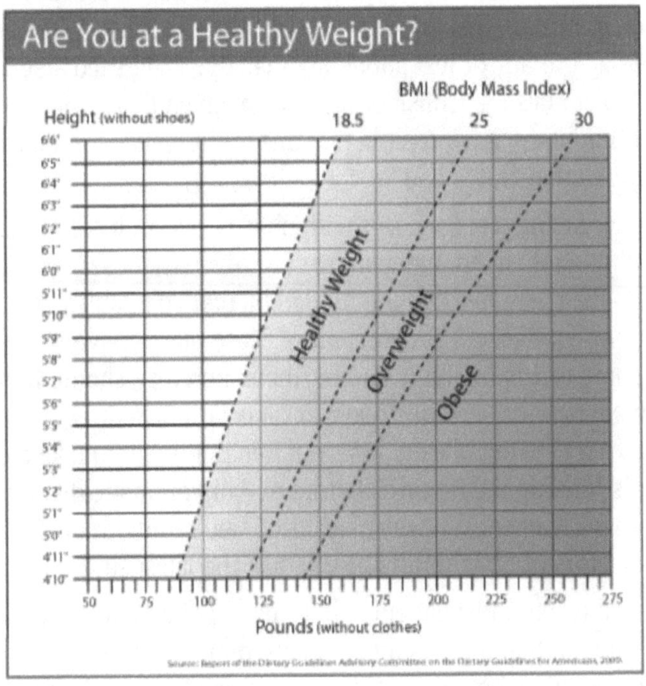

Locate your own BMI and you may be in for a surprise. As a heavy adult, I'm not surprised to find myself in the obese category. But my husband, who is lean and athletic, is overweight according to this chart. The point is to not be too stressed out by the "official" numbers.

The more important question to ask yourself is, "How does the person feel?" If your heavy teen is gasping for breath from walking up the stairs, there may be a problem. If he weighs 250 lbs and is the star of the football team, then weight may be less of a concern for your teen.

Health Concerns

Obesity is viewed as a real concern by most medical professionals. They point to increased incidences of diabetes, sleep apnea, asthma, high blood pressure and other physical issues created by the extra weight. In cases of extreme weight, there is no doubt that the burden of additional pounds can contribute to discomfort and disease.

However, history has shown that the most modern research isn't always accurate. Years ago, people believed the earth was flat. They believed that morphine was good for teething babies. They believed that mercury was a cure-all for just about any malady. They used arsenic to treat syphilis. The list goes on. Considering how much emphasis our society places on the ideal thin body, it is possible that this research has been biased in an attempt to prove that "fat is bad".

One of the biggest concerns with obesity research coming out today is funding. Although there are independent or university-based researchers, there are also many studies that are funded by diet companies, food companies, or pharmaceutical companies. These places have a vested interest in telling people that being fat is bad for them, and they should follow a certain diet, eat or avoid certain foods, or take a miracle drug to "cure" themselves. In reviewing obesity research it is important to take a careful look at who's funding the research before making dramatic dietary or lifestyle changes. Genetics, physical activity, and family traditions may be stronger indicators of your child's health than the latest study.

Several recent independent studies have pointed out that it is actually fitness, not weight, that matters most in determining a person's longevity[7]. In fact, many people who are considered overweight but are physically fit may have longer lifespans than those that are in the normal weight range[8]. Thus, there is no reason that we all need to fit into the same cookie cutter shape. This evidence suggests that breaking the mold may actually be better for you! As the bumper sticker says, "Why Be Normal?"

If your child is happy with who he is, even if he's not "normal," I encourage you to respect his choices and move on. Is he's unhappy, talk to him, engage with him, and help him make smart changes to enable him to get healthy. Talk about biking as an option. It opened up so many doors to me as a youth that I wish all teens could have the same positive experiences with bicycling. It's an unbeatable way to transform a body and a spirit.

How to Help your Teen Get Happy and Healthy Through Bicycling

There are many ways to help heavy teens, including encouraging diet, exercise, or a combination of the two. As I described earlier in the book, teens may be sensitive about their weight and, because they are teenagers, they may be particularly resistant to change. One of the best ways to get a teen to do something is to find an activity they love. Because of this, I believe that bicycling is a particularly wonderful option to help teens get happy and healthy. Biking is a great form of exercise for bigger riders, and provides many advantages that make it particularly appealing to teens.

I am a bigger bike rider myself – I've been through these things and understand the joys and challenges that go along with being a heavy biker. Because of that, I started my own business building and selling bikes for big riders (Zize Bikes). I hope you can learn from my experiences.

My Story

I was just a little overweight as an adolescent. I actually thought I was really fat, but when I look at pictures of myself, I realize that it was only in my mind that I was fat. I was NOT stick thin like most of my friends, but mildly overweight. Plump.

I was child number three of five, and very independent. I liked to get around on my own power so that I didn't have to be reliant on my mother or an older sibling to bring me places. When I was 14 I got a great bike--a bright red Columbia 10 speed! It was the coolest bike, and I rode it everywhere: my friends' houses (2-12 miles), the swimming hole (8 miles), the mall (4 miles), the park (3 miles), school (4 miles). I rode for the pure joy of it. I rode to blow off steam. I rode alone, I rode with my friends. My bike was my freedom and my life. It was an extension of myself.

With all my riding, a couple of things happened. First, I got strong, and fast. It wasn't intentional, I just pedaled--and moved--fast. When I'd ride with friends, I was always leading the pack. If there had been a cycling team in my town or at my school, I would have joined in a heartbeat, because I could outpace anybody on my bike. It wasn't done so much to be faster, but because I just loved that freedom, that feeling of flying, so much that it was an automatic response to climbing on my bike.

The other thing that happened was that I lost weight. My jeans got loose on me, and each time I'd get new ones, I'd regularly drop a size. I looked and felt great. I had good color, I was filled with joy, and I was able to go where ever I wanted whenever I wanted. I loved reaching out to people, feeling confident in myself and my ability. I transformed from an introverted, mostly insecure adolescent to a confident, self-assured young woman.

I share this story with you to give you hope. I was insecure, convinced I was fat, and uncoordinated. A bicycle helped me evolve into an active, confident woman who grew strong and trim without intending it. Because I loved my bike, and because I used it, my life changed. You can help your child create that kind of transformation, too. Her size or current physical fitness level doesn't matter. Her willingness to ride is all that matters. Everything else happens automatically.

Why Is a Bicycle a Good Choice?

Bike riding is an ideal activity for heavy teens. It offers physical advantages over other forms of exercise recommended and available to heavy individuals. Furthermore, the psychological and logistical advantages of biking (it's fun and provides a cheap mode of transportation) make it particularly well-suited for teenagers.

Biking is one of the few exercises that are non-weight bearing, which is especially important for heavy people. Many experts recommend walking as the ideal exercise, and I'll agree that it doesn't get much simpler than walking. However, while biking may not use as many muscles as walking, it has multiple advantages over walking.

If the exerciser is heavy, the strain of walking (particularly on hard pavement) can create a lot of damage to the ligaments. It can also lead to back pain, as the effort of remaining upright for an extended period of time can be stressful. On a bike you are seated, so there is no stress on your knees or repeated pressure on your joints. The motion of cycling builds up your leg muscles, and before you know it you're riding faster and with more ease than you might have thought possible.

Walking can also be a problem when the exerciser doesn't have a lot of time, and needs to combine actually getting somewhere with their exercise. Deciding to walk home from school following an after-school activity instead begging a parent or friend for a ride is a great idea, but between homework and curfew, your teen may not have an extra hour to spend walking. Instead, hopping on a bike and riding home is a fast and convenient alternative. It's also a great way to get to the store, or to a friend's house.

Another reason why biking is the ideal exercise for a heavy teen is that it is fun. How else can an overweight person move so fast totally on her own power? One push of the pedal and you've ridden 8 feet. It is a proven scientific fact that it is impossible to ride a bike and not smile. (Okay, that isn't a scientific fact, but it is the truth, in my opinion.) Even the moodiest teen will hop on a bike, start pedaling, feel the breeze, and start showing that child-like joy you may have thought was lost forever.

Bikes are also an environmentally friendly choice. They take no gas, no electricity, and no power other than the kind the rider makes himself. There are no problems with emissions and no pollution whatsoever from this mode of transportation.

Finally, biking is inexpensive. Once you purchase a bike, it costs almost nothing to use. Imagine the money saved on gas, parking, insurance, repairs, and public transportation! The right bike isn't necessarily inexpensive, but all it usually needs is an annual tune up and you can ride it for years. Take this in contrast to the cost of having your teen participate in organized sports. With membership fees, equipment, private lessons, etc., this could easily cost upwards of $200 per month. If your teen participated in a sport for all four years of high school that would add up to $9600! And that's not even including your time driving him to and from the activity. So consider a bike an investment that you may have to put a bit into now, but will pay off in the long run.

Go Solo or Join a Group

One of the many neat things about bike riding is that the rider can adapt it to the kind of activity he likes. Whether your teen is an introvert who likes quiet time or an extrovert who likes to meet new people, biking can work for him.

People who enjoy solo time spend their rides in a variety of possible activities. Some people like to take the time to enjoy the scenery and reach an almost meditative state. Some spend their time on a bike tracking their time, practicing sprinting, and working on increasing their speed. Other riders prefer to listen to some tunes while pedaling. (If this is what your teen likes, keep in mind that headphones can be dangerous because the rider can't hear traffic, so consider finding a music player or speakers she can put on her handlebars.)

In contrast, other people enjoy riding in groups. They may pick a meeting point and head out for a ride from there. Or they may have a starter who rides to one friend's house and picks him up. They ride together to the next rider's house, and when the group is all there, they head out on their adventure.

If you think your teen would prefer riding in groups but doesn't have anyone to ride with, many bike stores will coordinate local group rides. It's a great way for your teen to meet others with similar interests. There is usually an indication of the difficulty level of the ride, so you don't have to worry about your teen taking on dangerous rides beyond her skill level.

There are also many charity bike rides, which can be a fun and inspiring activity for either a single or group rider. A solo rider can collect donations and enjoy the ride by herself, while a more extroverted rider may want to join or form a team. Either way, there's the bonus of contributing to a worthy cause and getting in a fun ride, usually with great refreshments and support along the route.

Some of the more well-known charity bike rides that could be in your area are listed below. There are also many more.

American Diabetes Association Tour de Cure

Cycle for Life (Cystic Fibrosis)

MS Bike Rides (National Multiple Sclerosis Society)

AIDS Ride for Life

Another great option for an ambitious rider is joining a bike team. School-organized bike teams are becoming more and more common, especially in college athletics. For the rider who wants to really practice his speed, this can be a great way to build it up. Plus, team camaraderie increases youths' self-confidence and interpersonal skills. Your teen doesn't need years of experience in biking to join a team. A desire to do well and some hard work are often all it takes to excel. Furthermore, your teen may actually have an advantage, as bigger riders can often move fast going down hills, and lots of pedaling will build his leg muscles for strength on the flats and uphills. High school is a great time to start riding competitively because colleges often recruit their athletes in high school.

Choosing the Right Equipment

Bicycle prices range from $100 at big box stores to $5000 and over for extremely high-end frames and components. The bike that is the best fit for your teen depends on a number of factors. Since you've picked up this book, let's assume your teen is heavy. The question becomes, "How heavy?"

Any person who weighs more than 200 pounds should use extreme caution in selecting a bicycle. Most manufacturers build bikes that only hold 200 pounds. This is not to say that people who weigh more than 200 pounds shouldn't ride--they should (everybody should if you ask me)! But they need to be careful. If your daughter is 5'9" and weighs 180 pounds, she'll be fine on most bikes. If she gets much heavier, you probably need to start taking some of the following points into consideration when selecting a bicycle for her.

A word of caution here: your teen may have some shame around her weight. As I discussed earlier in the book, our culture worships thinness so much that even naturally thin people obsess about the number on the scale. In helping your teen get healthy by offering her a bike, I caution you not to become too rigid in your assessment of her needs. You can ask how much she weighs, but don't be surprised if she doesn't want to tell you. She may even lie about her weight. So take your best guess about what she weighs. If you think it's over 200 pounds, or if she's gaining weight rapidly, be sure to select a bike that can hold more weight.

If you invest in a bike that is not strong enough, the bike will break. Repeatedly. It will not encourage riding. It will not be safe. It is not worth it to save some money, when the whole reason you're doing this is to help your child succeed. Every penny you invest in a bike that your child loves will be returned to you multiple times as you watch him get stronger, trim down, make new friends, develop self-confidence and independence (and maybe even develop a life away from the TV and computer).

Things to Consider for a Strong Bicycle

Through much trial and error on my own and with a team of engineers at Zize Bikes, I have discovered several key features that are crucial to getting a strong bike that can hold a bigger rider. Please, for the sake of your teen and your wallet, take these into account when selecting a bike for your child.

1. Steel's the Deal

The bike frame is the base of the bike, and is crucial to its strength. There's a lot of discussion among bikers about what the ideal frame material is. Many argue that steel is too heavy and aluminum is equally good and much lighter. This is true, but only to a point. Today, most of the materials chosen for bikes are selected to make the bike lighter. While this may suit the racing community, it does not always suit the everyday rider. In contrast, chromoly steel gives a very smooth and compliant ride, while having the ability to meet heavier riders' needs for a strong frame. This is important because if the frame should crack, it could cause serious injury to the rider. Steel could conceivably bend, but it won't crack.

2. Strong Rims and Spokes

Rims and spokes are not often noticed by the everyday bike shopper but they are crucial to safely support the weight of a bigger rider. The rims need to be thick and wide, and the more spokes, the better. Many bikes have 32 spokes, but if you can find one with 36, this is much better. The spokes themselves need to be really strong as well. I suggest stainless steel spokes. The nickel found in stainless steel makes them stronger than thicker, all steel spokes. Stainless steel also has the advantage of never rusting—one less thing to worry about.

3. Hefty Tires

One of the most obvious problems heavy riders face when getting on a bike is that the tires quickly deflate. The solution to that problem is to get wide, sturdy tires. These hold more air and provide a more cushioned ride without the frequent, ongoing risk of getting flat tires.

4. High Thread Count Tires

In addition to width, another important factor in tires is the thread count. A high thread count is crucial to the sturdiness of the tire itself. Think of the difference between gauzy material and woolen blanket. A hire thread count tire, like a woolen blanket, does a better job of hold the air in and holding the rider up. Which would you want to be responsible for holding your teen?

5. Put the Metal in the Pedal

Because a big rider's push is stronger, their pedals also need to be stronger. The hard plastic pedals that are usually found on inexpensive bicycles often fall or break off. A lightweight aluminum pedal may be ideal for a road racer, but it is often not strong enough for plus sized riders. What a big rider needs is a strong, wide, metal pedal, with a strong bearing system.

6. Get Cranky

The crank, the arms and chain ring that the pedals attach to, is one of the components most frequently damaged by heavy riders on regular bikes. This, when you think about it, makes a lot of sense. After all, this is where the riders puts all of his weight. Especially for people who stand up and ride, a heavier person can easily destroy a less-than-solid crank. In searching for a bike for a big rider, look for a crank of highest quality. Be sure to ask the seller what weight it's rated for. Look for thicker metal, welded or forged parts, and, quite frankly, a higher cost. While paying a lot does not always mean you get quality, with bicycle parts you really do get what you pay for.

7. A Bulge Bar

Another important thing for bigger riders to look for is a large, wide handlebar and clamping system (where the handlebar clamps on to the handlebar stem). I suggest a bulge bar that has a 3.18 mm clamping area and a 31.8 mm handlebar stem. This combination provides maximum strength.

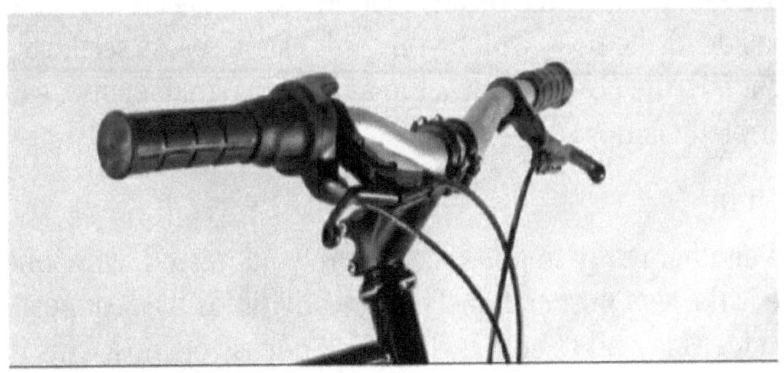

8. A Comfortable Seat (They exist--really!)

I won't get any disagreement on this one, I'm sure. There are very few people I know who say that they find bike saddles comfortable, because most are not. Originally designed merely as a place to briefly rest your bottom while riding, today most recreational bikers use the saddle as a seat. Comfort is crucial. Your teen may want to try out several seats, as each will feel different, depending on her sit bones. Look for a wide seat that is well padded. Gel is often used as a comfortable addition.

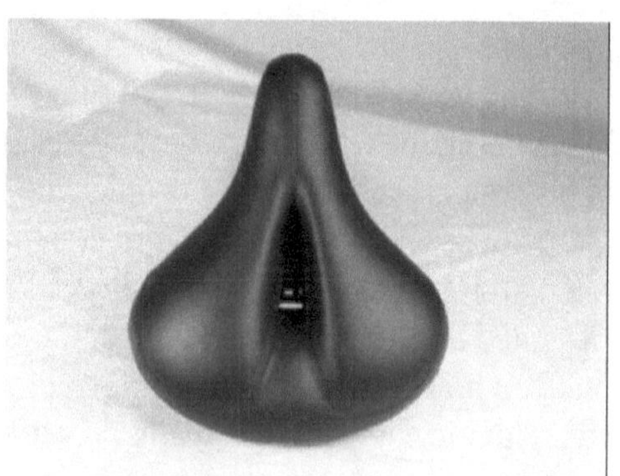

9. Avoid Wiggly Seats

Most of the rider's weight will be on the bike seat, so in addition to it being comfortable, you want to be sure that it's not going anywhere. The seat clamp is what attaches the seat to the post of the bike. A strong bike will have an integrated seat post, which means that the clamp is actually a part of the post. The inside of the post, which you can't easily see, is serrated, and locks the seat right into the post. You want to avoid a separate clamp, even a separate serrated clamp.

10. Clamp It In

Yet another really important, but rarely addressed, component of a strong bike is the seat post clamp. This actually holds the seat post in place on the bicycle. Many bikes come with quick release clamps. This is great because it makes changing the seat height easier, but it may cause problems for anyone of substantial size. It's not that it will release while you're riding, but you may find that your seat slides without your touching it. Avoid this by getting a strong clamp that is not quick-release. For example, at Zize Bikes we double bolt our seat post clamps -- we mean business.

If you'd like a handy list for comparing bikes when you shop, visit our website for a free download[9].

Riding Safely

Hopefully once your teen gets her bike, she'll be so excited that you'll wonder when you'll see her again. Not to worry -- she'll be back for food and drink, if nothing else! However, before you set her loose, there are a few things you should do. They are safety checks, if you will, which will ensure that your teen will be safe and that you can relax.

Rules of the Road

If your child already drives, then he has a huge advantage, since cyclists follow the same rules of the road as cars. (Yes, this includes stopping at stop signs, giving pedestrians the right of way, and always being alert.) If your child doesn't drive yet, please download "Bicycle Rules of the Road," which was created by the Illinois Traffic Safety Division[10]. It's an excellent synopsis of safe driving rules, and applies to cyclists everywhere. Encourage your child to read it and learn it. Not only will it help him be a better cyclist, but it will also make getting his driver's license a lot easier!

Along with following the rules of the road, it's important for your teen to incorporate the following techniques into his riding skills.

Be conspicuous. Ride so drivers can see you.

Anticipate the actions of drivers, other cyclists, and pedestrians . For example, if you see a car pull over to the side of the road, don't ride too close--somebody's probably going to open the door shortly.

Stay cool and collected. Don't get angry or vengeful towards drivers. Cars are bigger and have a motor. The biker will always be the loser in those battles.

Always check that your tires are well inflated before you head out. Riding on insufficient air will damage your bike and make it a lot harder to ride. This is true for everybody, but essential for big riders.

Important Accessories

There are a few accessories that I consider essential for safety and comfort. Some of these will keep your child safe from cars, some from vandals, and some will prevent your child from multitasking, which can be just as dangerous as external threats.

1. A helmet . Get a good helmet that your teen will wear. There are lots of different styles and designs out there, so find one your teen loves. Simple or funky, racer or cap, it doesn't matter. Just get one that he likes, and require that he wear it. Helmets save lives.

2. A light. Although most teens probably won't spend much time riding at night, you never know. An even more dangerous time is at dusk, when the kids think they can see fine, but the cars actually have a very difficult time seeing them. Every bike should come with reflectors, but invest in lights on the front and rear of the bike, too. It can help the rider avoid pot holes and allow vehicles to spot him easily.

3. A lock. Your environment will dictate how serious of a lock you need to invest in, but get one. Even in small towns people may be tempted by an unwatched bike. In cities people can and do saw through locks and steal parts off bikes. Buy what's necessary for your environment. Whether the lock serves as a deterrent for somebody going on a joy ride or is serious enough to stop a real criminal, it's important to always lock the bike when not in use.

4. A basket or rack. Secure a rack on the back of the bike or put a basket on the front—whichever is preferred. That way your teen will never be caught trying to juggle riding with one hand and an arm full of books or a bag of groceries. Being well prepared can prevent accidents.

5. A water bottle holder and a water bottle. Kind of obvious, but everyone needs help remembering the simplest things. Your child needs to stay hydrated, so make it easy for her.

Make a Contract for Success

A good bike is an investment. Like any investment, you need to treat it with respect. If you present the new bicycle to your teen with an agreement about its use, you'll feel confident that your child is riding safely, your investment will be well-protected, and you'll feel good about helping him succeed. A signed contract can go a long way in creating success for your teen. As a bonus, it will give you guidance for any consequences you may have to consider.

Here are some suggestions of points you may want to include in your agreement (this is also available in a free downloadable form online[11]).

Agreement for the Use of Your Teen's Bicycle Between __________ (parent) and __________ (child)

_____It is my bike. I bought it. I paid for it. I am loaning it to you. Aren't I the greatest?

_____When the bike is stored anywhere other than our closed garage, you will lock it. Always. I will have the combination or a copy of the key.

_____You will wear a properly fitted helmet whenever you ride the bike. Even around the block.

_____You will learn the rules of the road for cyclists. You will follow these rules at all times.

_____When there is an option to use a bike path, you will use it.

_____You will not engage in dangerous behavior while on your bike (e.g., racing your friends in cars). You will always ride single file when on a street and pay attention to your surroundings.

_____If the bike disappears or is smashed, by you or by someone you lent it to, you are responsible for the replacement costs or repairs.

_____When you need to go somewhere, think of riding your bike before you ask for a ride. This will keep you independent and fit.

_____Let me know when you're heading out for a ride.

_____When you ride at dusk or at night, always use your lights. Even though you can see them, cars cannot see you well, and they are a lot bigger than you are.

_____Open up your eyes. See the world happening around you. Check out the scenery when you go for a ride. Listen to the birds. Ride to the lake and take a swim. Invite a new kid in school to go on a ride with you. Enjoy.

_____You will mess up. I will take away your bike. We will sit down and talk about it. We will start over again. You and I, we are always learning. I am on your team. We are in this together.

Summary

For teens, biking is a blast. For the motivated obese teen, biking can be a life saver. A few of the main points I hope you will take away from this book are listed below.

1. Let go of the blame and shame. Forgive yourself for any non-perfect parenting you've done, and focus on the present.

2. Enroll your teen, if there's interest. Help your teen get excited about reclaiming his or her life. Work with him or her to create a home environment that is conducive to getting in shape.

3. Recognize health concerns for what they are and what they are not. Being heavy and in shape is fine (and according to some studies even healthier than being of normal weight). However, major obesity and inactivity are associated with health problems and may be cause for concern.

4. Bicycle riding is the ideal exercise for heavy teens. Bicycling is a great non-weight bearing exercise, it's good for the environment, and bikes cost nothing to use. They're a fast means of transportation and can be used alone or in a group. Best of all, they can incredibly freeing (especially for teens trying to gain their independence).

5. Choose the right bicycle . The rider's weight has a lot to do with how well the bike will hold up. If your teen is heavy, you should look for a steel frame and strong, reinforced components for a solid, comfortable, and safe ride.

6. Ride safely. Teens (and all riders) should be aware of and follow the cycling rules of the road.

7. Contract for bicycle use. One great way to connect with your child and supervise their riding is to develop a contract with your teen for the safe use and maintenance of the bike.

Additional Resources

The League of American Bicyclists is an outstanding organization whose mission is to promote bicycling for fun, fitness, transportation and work through advocacy and education for a bicycle-friendly America. Among other things, they provide tips for better and smarter cycling, and classes for cyclists.